willing walkers

willing walkers

The Story of Dogs for the Blind

GORDON CARTER

With an introduction
by
Arthur J. Phillipson
Guide Dogs for the Blind, London

Abelard-Schuman *london new york toronto*

by the same author:

WHITE HARNESSES

MASTERS AND MASTERPIECES OF MUSIC

LONDON Abelard-Schuman Limited 8 King Street WC2
NEW YORK Abelard-Schuman Limited 6 West 57 Street
TORONTO Abelard-Schuman Canada Limited 896 Queen Street West
© *Gordon Carter 1965*
first published 1965
Library of Congress Catalogue Card Number 65-10774

contents

U. S. 1327893

illustrations

[8]

foreword

Guide Dogs are being trained in greater numbers every year, and this book helps to tell the public, and particularly children, about the wonderful job they are doing. A dog when working in its white harness – guiding its blind master – should never be petted or distracted from its job as it requires all its concentration for the important work it has in hand.

It is perhaps hard for people who have always had their sight to realize just what it means for a blind person to go to work, or even just for a walk, without asking for aid from somebody else – or by tapping their way along slowly and conspicuously with a white stick. With a Guide Dog they can walk as fast as most people and few passers-by know that they are blind.

But, please remember that a Guide Dog's life is not all work. After the short time it spends in harness each day it leads the normal life of a fit and contented dog for the rest of the day.

The training of Guide Dogs is being undertaken in several countries and this book helps to show how the movement first started and developed. It also deals with all the aspects of a Guide Dog's life, right from its puppyhood and through its working life. It is a book that is full of interest and shows the amazing partnership that can develop between a blind person and his dog.

Arthur Phillipson

Chief Controller of Training,
The Guide Dogs for the Blind Association

1: a clever dog

Towards the end of the First World War (1914-18) a German soldier who had been wounded and blinded in battle was in a German Military Hospital. One day he was outside in the grounds with a young German doctor who was helping him to walk around. People who have not been blind for long do not find it easy to move about, even in quiet places, unless there is somebody kind enough to guide them.

The young doctor was called away for a short time, but he was thoughtful enough to leave his pet dog with the soldier so that he would not be lonely.

When the doctor returned he was dismayed to discover that

his dog and the blind patient were not where he had left them. He looked around and called for them. When he found them he was naturally puzzled to know how they had managed by themselves. The soldier said that the dog had guided him along the paths.

The young doctor thought this was most unusual because his dog was only a pet and had never been taught to do anything for anybody. He wondered what would happen if a dog of a working strain were to be trained to guide a blind man. He decided to find out. The success of what he was patient enough to do became known to the German Government. It was decided to train dogs to help blind soldiers.

When the war had ended, an American and his wife, George and Dorothy Eustis, went to Switzerland to breed and train German shepherd dogs, or alsatians as they are called in Great Britain. Quite by chance, they learned what was happening in Germany as a result of the actions of the German doctor and his dogs. Dorothy Eustis and her husband saw trained dogs guiding blind men at Potsdam. Mrs. Eustis described what she saw in a letter which she sent to an American magazine.

This book is about the events that followed.

2 : the adventure begins

One early evening in the town of Nashville, Tennessee, a young man walked out of an insurance office after finishing a day's work. He was tired and he looked forward to going home. It was late November, 1927, and a cold wind was blowing. He pulled up his coat collar to keep his face warm.

Morris Frank was no ordinary young man. He was blind and, like many blind people, he had to be assisted across the street by a friend. He was just about to begin an adventure which was to change his whole life.

. "*Evening Post,* Mr. Frank?" a friendly magazine seller

asked. "There is a story inside about how dogs are helping blind people. You will find it most interesting."

News about blind people was of great importance to Morris. He always hoped that he would learn something to help him. Things had never been the same since he lost his sight. It was so difficult to live a normal life. He bought the magazine gladly.

As soon as he had arrived home Morris asked his parents to find the story in the magazine and read it to him.

"Yes, here it is – it's a letter written by a Mrs. Dorothy Eustis and it is headed 'The Seeing Eye'."

Morris listened carefully as his father read it. Dorothy Eustis explained how she had been to Potsdam in Germany to visit a school where Police Dogs were trained. To her surprise, she had seen dogs being trained to help soldiers who had been blinded in the First World War. She had watched dogs and blind men walking together along the streets, across main roads, and up and down steps, and all in perfect safety. She had hardly believed her eyes at first, but it was really true. Dogs and blind men together could do wonderful things.

Morris Frank was filled with a new hope. He wanted to know more about the splendid work. Indeed, he would like a dog like that for himself. He decided to ask his parents to write a letter to Mrs. Eustis.

"Why, Morris, the address isn't in the United States at all! The lady lives in Switzerland."

"Never mind, perhaps Mrs. Eustis knows where dogs like

those are being trained over here," was his answer. So Morris Frank's letter was sent and he waited impatiently for a reply.

On the day a letter came with a Swiss postmark there was a tremendous air of excitement in Morris's home. The young blind man listened even more attentively than to the magazine's story.

How pleasant it was to hear from him, wrote Mrs. Eustis. There were no guide dogs in America. As far as she knew the dogs at Potsdam were the only ones. She and her husband, George, however, trained dogs of their own. They bred them and trained them for farmers, the Swiss police, and the Red Cross. They could perhaps try to train one just for him, but she would like to meet him first. He would need to go to Switzerland to meet the dog and learn how to use it. Would he be willing? She would be in New York for Christmas if he was still interested. They could talk about it then.

Morris Frank met Mrs. Eustis, and it was arranged that he should go to Switzerland when she sent for him. She explained that a dog would have to be specially chosen. Then it would have to be trained by an American friend who was helping her in Switzerland, Elliott Humphrey. He would need at least three months to teach the dog its tasks: how to cross in traffic; how to wait at the edge of pavements; how to guide his owner up and down steps, and other things as well. She would have to find a willing dog – one willing to be taught and willing to serve. Morris would have to be patient until all these things were done.

[15]

After Mrs. Eustis had returned to Switzerland and the weeks passed, the young man did not find it easy to be patient. In Switzerland, Dorothy and her husband, George, and Elliott Humphrey, were busy watching the alsatians which were about the correct age for training as Guide Dogs. After a few weeks they chose a handsome young bitch called " Kiss ". Elliott Humphrey began training her, together with another dog to keep her company.

Kiss had to learn to carry out Elliott's kindly words of command. She was taught to *sit*, to *lie down*, to *stay* and *come* when called. She had to walk without pulling or slowing down unexpectedly. Each day she learned a bit more and became more expert in her lessons. She had to move around dangerous objects in her path which might strike Morris: trees, poles, fences, railings and boxes which people left carelessly outside their homes.

Some months went by, and finally the day came when Morris was asked to go to Switzerland. His dog was ready to meet him.

The young blind man had a grand send-off. His relations, friends, and newspaper reporters who had heard of the strange adventure, all went with him to New York to see him off on his trip to Europe. The only person to believe that a dog really could help a blind person was Morris himself.

The sea voyage to Europe was a tonic to somebody whose life had been so limited by blindness. Morris was still young enough to be ready to fight against his handicap. By the time

[16]

the ship had crossed the Atlantic Ocean, and he had journeyed across France by train, he was feeling tired, but more prepared to face any challenges.

Dorothy Eustis and her friends were at Lausanne to meet him. She took his arm and began to answer his numerous questions.

"Our home, Fortunate Fields we call it, is only a short distance now. We will soon be there. Your dog is a most handsome German shepherd – a bitch with a beautiful grey coat and a flash on her throat."

"A bitch?" asked Morris in surprise.

"Yes, a bitch," laughed his companion. "Females can be helpful sometimes, you know."

On his arrival at Fortunate Fields the blind insurance salesman was eager to meet his dog. The introduction was to be made by Elliott Humphrey, who was quietly studying Morris's personality and his physical mannerisms. It was his job to match the dog with the man, and he could not know enough about either of them.

"Her name is Kiss," said Mr. Humphrey.

Morris was stroking Kiss and feeling over her majestic body.

"This is no Kiss – she is much too proud for that name! I shall re-name her Buddy, because we are going to be friends."

Training Buddy and Morris together took place for many hours each day for several weeks. Morris had to learn the way to give Buddy orders. They had to be short so that she could

[17]

understand them, and they had to be firm so that she would never become confused. *Left* and *right*, *forward* and *stay* were some of the important ones. Morris had to learn how to attract Buddy's attention if ever it began to wander. *Hup, hup* said encouragingly was the expression he used.

They had many adventures during training. Two were so special that Morris Frank realized that he would have little to fear when Buddy and he were in the streets of New York.

One day Buddy and Morris and their watchful trainer were proceeding along a narrow country lane. On each side the grass banks rose sharply and steeply. Mr. Humphrey was walking farther behind Morris than usually, proudly eyeing the steady improvement in his handling of his dog.

Suddenly, he heard the terrifying sound of runaway horses coming down the track towards them. He was too far behind to be able to help. All he could do was to shout a warning.

Morris heard the horses and the shout, but he had no idea that Buddy and he were in a cutting between steep slopes. He froze in fear and uncertainty. His dog had heard the thundering hooves and decided to act quickly. She pulled her master to one side of the lane and dragged him sharply up the side of the hill. Dog and blind man held on to each other as a team of runaway horses and a cart pounded around the bend and dashed along the path they had just left.

On another occasion Morris was tired after a day's training. He was resting in a chair, and feeling rather discouraged. There seemed so much to learn that he couldn't help wonder-

Morris Frank with Buddy

ing if he would ever be able to manage when Elliott Humphrey wasn't by his side to tell him what to do. Dorothy Eustis
found him quiet, weary, and sad.

"I would like to have a haircut," Morris said, "but I don't
feel like asking anybody to take me."

"Why not go alone with Buddy tomorrow?" Mrs. Eustis
challenged him. "You are both doing so well that it will cheer
you up to know you can do something by yourselves. I will
explain how to get there."

The thought of going somewhere without his trainer by
his side made Morris feel extremely nervous. He knew Mrs.
Eustis was right. If only he could do this alone, then he would
have more hope and courage for the future.

When Morris Frank started out the next day he was the
first blind American to walk out into the unknown accom-
panied by only a trained dog. He was making his way in the
darkness of the blind with Buddy as his eyes. He spoke to her,
encouraged her, and gave his orders clearly, although he was
trembling inside. He wondered if she guessed how he felt.
They managed very well and returned to Fortunate Fields full
of joy.

"It's wonderful!" exclaimed the young man. "If only
other blind people could have dogs like my Buddy."

"When you return to the United States and show how well
you manage, I will do all I can to help others," promised
Dorothy Eustis.

The friends at Fortunate Fields were sorry when it was

time for the young man to leave them, but they kept their thoughts to themselves, for they wanted the parting to be a happy occasion. They had all done their best and the future now rested with Buddy and her owner. There was nothing more that could be done for them.

Morris knew he felt much better than when he had arrived. The fresh air and exercise had made him fit again. The training had been more difficult than he had imagined, but he had succeeded. He was looking forward to the days ahead. He and Buddy were full of confidence. The ship was waiting for them both and the gangway was the bridge between Switzerland and America.

"Forward, Buddy," said the young man. "Good girl."

3: Morris and Buddy in New York

When Morris Frank walked off the ship at New York with his new friend Buddy, he was surprised to find newspaper reporters and photographers waiting for him. Some of them did not believe that a man could be guided by a dog, and said so.

" Let us see what your dog can do, Mr. Frank," one of them demanded.

Morris, tired after his voyage, was dismayed by the request, but he knew he would have to demonstrate for his onlookers. Any stories which were printed in American newspapers would be really about the work of Dorothy Eustis and her friends. He must be ready to do his best for their sakes.

Buddy had no fears and took Morris through the crowds on the dockside as calmly as if they were in the quiet lanes of Switzerland. The reporters followed with cameras clicking, and the party made their way to the busy street. Even in 1928 there was a steady flow of traffic. Morris could feel the eyes following them. He stroked his dog's head as they prepared to meet their first big test in the United States.

"Forward!" He quietly gave the order to cross the high way. There were no pedestrian crossings or traffic lights to help them. Morris had to cross without any warning for the truck drivers who were surprised to see a man and dog suddenly leave the pavement. They had no idea he was blind and could not see them. Buddy had to stop more than once, and it seemed ages before they reached the safety of the other side. Morris was quite shaken when they arrived.

"Well done!" complimented an admiring reporter.

Morris Frank knew, however, that he would need lots of practice in New York's traffic before Buddy and he dare show themselves to the general public. In the days that followed he made many crossings of the busy streets until he became expert and he could go anywhere with confidence. He then sent a telegram to Dorothy Eustis in Switzerland.

"Just put one word – *success*," he told the clerk.

"Is that all? Just *success*?" asked the puzzled man.

"Yes, that is all," smiled Morris. He was certain Mrs. Eustis

Morris Frank crossing a street

would know what he meant. He and Buddy were ready to meet New York and its problems.

The first task was to find work. If he could earn his own living this would prove to others that a blind man need not be helpless. He could look after himself like men and women who were able to see. He decided to try for a job helping blind people like himself. It was not easy to find anybody who would employ him. How would a blind man be able to visit other blind people in their homes and help them with their difficulties? This was what greeted Morris at the offices where he tried to find a job.

Finally, his patience was exhausted, and he decided to return to his insurance business. He was determined to prove himself as useful as other men who worked for their living. Back in Nashville, he soon became a familiar figure with his famous dog. Many called him by his name.

"Good morning, Morris."

"How are you doing, Mr. Frank?"

These friendly voices were like music to his ears, for there was no hint of pity in their greetings. His friend now greeted him like anybody else. Buddy had already worked wonders.

On one occasion Morris and his dog had a shock. The news that a dog show was to be held gave Morris the idea that this would be a chance to meet other people who owned dogs. It would be pleasant to talk with animal lovers, and he had no doubt that Buddy would be the star of the show. Unfortunately, Buddy had too many admirers who had given her tit-

[25]

bits. This kind of attention was bad for her and she was not in top condition. Buddy, indeed, was a bit too fat. This was what the judges thought, and no prize was given to her.

The spectators at the ringside were upset by the decision and began to murmur disapproval.

" How can a dog as clever as that not be considered good enough for a prize? Disgraceful! " One angry lady was plainly heard by all, including the judges. It was obvious that a difficult situation had arisen. All ended happily when it was decided to award a special prize for the best dog from overseas. As Buddy was the only one, to the delight of all those present she won the prize. Even so, her master was more careful in future about his dog being given extra rations.

Every day Morris and Buddy went out to try to interest people in insurance. Nashville, Morris's home town, was soon to be the scene of a great deal of excitement. Morris had received letters from blind people asking how they could get dogs like Buddy, whose fame had spread. The young man wrote to Mrs. Eustis and told her of these inquiries. She replied that she would be willing to train more dogs. She would come to the United States to start a school where the blind could learn how to use them.

Early in 1929 Dorothy Eustis returned to America to start The Seeing Eye. She interested her relatives and some of her friends in her plans and managed to raise some money. Morris opened an office which was to be the headquarters. A friend of Mr. Humphrey's, Willi Ebeling, had been enlisted as a helper. He lived in New Jersey where he bred and trained German shepherd dogs. He was eager to learn all about the work and became a tireless supporter of The Seeing Eye.

Nashville received a number of blind people who were trained with dogs sent from Fortunate Fields in Switzerland. The faithful Mr. Humphrey came over to do for them what he had done for Morris Frank. He was watched by his old friend, Willi Ebeling, who learned all he could as he saw miracles performed in the streets of the town.

There was one difficulty, however. It was very hot in Tennessee in the summer months. The heat was tiring for the blind people who had been inactive for so long. Tired people do not always give of their best and are exposed to danger if they cannot concentrate properly. Dogs walk rather quickly for weary students and this worried Dorothy Eustis. A different place would have to be found for The Seeing Eye.

Willi Ebeling came to the rescue. He already owned kennels of his own near Dover, New Jersey. He had German shepherd dogs as well. Why not move The Seeing Eye to his home? Why not indeed! The offer was greeted with joy and enthusiasm. Nobody was more pleased than the generous Willi Ebeling.

The climate of New Jersey was much more pleasant for both the blind people and the dogs. The trainers, too, were much happier, for they had been forced to toil in the heat of Nashville like everybody else. Willi Ebeling gave his house, kennels and dogs for more than two years. The blind students and their dogs lived in a small hotel in the town. They didn't escape without their share of excitement. One night a fire broke out. Before the fire engines had arrived the dogs had helped to take the students out of the building.

The move to New Jersey was a success, but the branches of The Seeing Eye were still spread far and wide. Some of the dogs were being bred and trained in Switzerland. Morris Frank was working at his office in Nashville. The hotel and kennels were some distance apart. In 1932 all this was changed when a large house with its own grounds a few miles outside Morristown was taken over by the hard-working friends.

Some of the local residents heard that big dogs would soon be living nearby. They didn't like the idea at all. They expected that the barking would be a nuisance. They were afraid that their own pets might be attacked, and perhaps even their children frightened. The Seeing Eye, however, arrived in 1932 and was able to make peace with the local residents.

In Europe and America, Mrs. Eustis, a handful of friends, and blind young Morris Frank and Buddy had started a snowball. The Seeing Eye had rolled so fast that other countries were touched by its amazing story.

4 : guide dogs come to England

News of the deeds of The Seeing Eye dogs had been reported by the newspapers in England. The *Liverpool Echo* printed articles and letters which were read by people who loved dogs, and also by people who were working to help the blind.

Among the many people who read the stories were two ladies who bred and trained alsatians or German shepherds: Muriel Crooke and Lady Kitty Ritson. They were interested and wanted to know more. So did Mr. Musgrave Frankland who lived in Liverpool, where he worked for the National Institute for the Blind. They decided to write to Dorothy Eustis and ask her to meet them in London. They listened carefully to Mrs. Eustis as she told them what they would have to do.

"You will need some kennels near to a large town or city. The country will not do because Guide Dogs need practice where there are many people and vehicles. You will need a good trainer and intelligent dogs, and, of course, some money."

Dorothy Eustis looked at them. She saw that her listeners were upset when she had finished talking.

"What is worrying you?" she asked. "I hoped to make you cheerful, not sad."

"Oh dear, we didn't expect it to be so difficult. We have no money, and no kennels near a city," one of them said.

"Nor do we know of anybody who can train Guide Dogs. We don't even have the experience to tell which dogs would be good eyes for the blind," another added.

"Oh, is that all?" smiled their guest. "I think I can put some of that right. If I give you the help of one of my trainers he will choose the dogs and train them for you. Will you do the rest?" All three agreed that they would. They left London smiling with pleasure at having taken a first step to help the blind of England.

Dorothy Eustis kept her promise. It was Elliott Humphrey who arrived in England in 1931. Muriel Crooke and her friends had not been idle. They had hired some wooden garages at New Brighton, in Cheshire, very near to the big city of Liverpool. They had sold flowers and vegetables from their gardens and started a small fund. They were very pleased with their efforts. They even wrote letters asking people to send money.

Elliott Humphrey was delighted with what they had done. Mrs. Crooke had asked breeders for dogs, alsatians, from which he could make a choice. With the exception of one, which cost only a few pounds, they were all given free. He chose the best and managed to train four blind men with them.

" It is simply wonderful since I had my dog," one of the blind men remarked. " I feel absolutely safe and would not be afraid to go anywhere now." Muriel Crooke and her friends knew that all their hard work had been amply rewarded. Soon, they received requests from blind men and women from all parts of England. " Please, may I have a Guide Dog too? " most of them wanted to know.

Elliott Humphrey, who had returned to Switzerland, was asked to come back and train more dogs. He came gladly, proud that the first dogs he had trained in England had done so well.

The next dogs he trained were just as good. Everybody was amazed at the new hope they gave to their blind owners. More people began to hear about their deeds and sent money to help.

It was decided that England must have a trainer all of her own. Captain Liakhoff, a Russian, was selected personally by Dorothy Eustis. He did so well that he stayed in England for the rest of his life and was awarded the Order of the British Empire for his work.

Muriel Crooke and her friends now had more helpers. "We need a name so that everybody will know what to do," somebody suggested one day.

It was agreed that this would be an excellent idea. They knew that the blind people in the United States were proud of the name of The Seeing Eye. It would be difficult for them to find one as good. Various names were considered until somebody suggested the Guide Dogs for the Blind of Great Britain. Everybody thought that this was a wonderful title.

In those early years the dogs were all alsatians. There were two reasons for this.

In the first place, Dorothy Eustis, her trainer and all the English pioneers were alsatian admirers and experts. They would never have dreamed of using any other kind of dog. Secondly, there were many alsatians in England from which to choose, as they were very popular between the two World Wars. Indeed, it was during the First World War that they began to arrive in England. They came in a most unusual way.

The German Army was using alsatians as messengers and Red Cross dogs in the front line. They were very clever. They had been trained to find the scent of human beings left wounded on the battlefield. When they made a discovery, they hurried back to their masters and guided them to the soldiers needing help. Messenger dogs had been taught to obey two masters. One was in the front line, and the other at

[32]

Six-week-old puppies being fed in the puppy kennels
at the Seeing Eye Breeding Farm

headquarters. The alsatians knew both their masters well and would take messages from one to the other when told to do so.

British soldiers sometimes captured the dogs. They became so attached to them that they brought them home with them after the war. They became very popular among their English owners. It is hardly surprising that they made such good Guide Dogs.

When the Second World War broke out in 1939, the Army asked people to lend their clever alsatians for training, just as the Germans had done before. There were now very few of the best alsatians left for Guide Dog duties, and the Guide Dogs for the Blind became anxious. They had opened their first Training Centre at Leamington Spa, in Warwickshire, and needed more good dogs than ever. The only thing they could do was to try out other breeds and see how they responded to training.

Fortunately, England had clever dogs of her own. They were carrying out tasks quite as astounding as the majestic alsatians. A chance to help the blind was about to be given to them.

There are very few people in England who have not heard about the collies and the way they help farmers to round up sheep. The trainers of the Guide Dogs knew all about them and decided to experiment with them.

The handsome black and white collies did wonderfully well and proved to be quick pupils. The best were not easy to purchase, however, for farmers needed intelligent and willing collies on the lonely hills in Wales and Scotland, where sheep roam for many miles. Retrievers were called into service, and the Labrador retrievers were found to be most reliable. Nearly all the Guide Dogs in England now are Labradors. Today the number of Guide Dog owners has increased from the first four to over one thousand. There are three Training Centres in England, at Leamington Spa, Exeter and Bolton, and a new one has recently been opened at Forfar, in Scotland.   U. S. 1327893

The cost of training each dog is over £250. The blind men and women may not be able to raise such a large amount, but this does not prevent them from obtaining a dog. They are asked to pay no more than they are able to afford. This may be as little as a few shillings, but most are able to manage a few pounds. The rest of the money is paid out of the funds of the Guide Dogs for the Blind Association.

The Seeing Eye also believes that blind people want to pay their own way in the world. A sum of $150 is asked towards the cost of the dog, board and lodging, equipment and training, and every applicant is treated in the same way. If it is for any reason difficult to pay this sum all at once, an arrangement can be made to pay over a period. This may be as little as a dollar a month.

Nobody, either in Britain or the United States, is refused a dog if they really cannot afford to pay anything at all. Blind people, however, are usually only too pleased and proud to bear some of the cost of their future freedom.

5: puppies and puppy walking

Changes have taken place since Elliott Humphrey trained the first alsatians in Switzerland and America. In Morristown, New Jersey. The Seeing Eye now has a breeding farm of its own where a team of experts see that there is a regular supply of the best alsatian puppies. In Great Britain the Guide Dogs for the Blind buy many of their puppies, usually Labrador retrievers, from reliable breeders throughout the land.

All these puppies are, of course, inoculated so that they are protected against diseases. As they aproach about ten weeks of age they are watched carefully to make certain they will become good guides. Healthy, friendly puppies usually like to romp and play. A puppy which showed any obvious shyness or temper would need to be watched. If either of these signs

[36]

continued, then a kind home might have to be found for it.

Many dogs dislike cats. Cats have to watch out when dogs are around, and may have to rush to the nearest tree or book-case for safety. Guide Dog puppies should be so friendly that they would never dream of behaving in such a way. There are many cats kept in Britain and the United States, and some blind people are fond of them and keep them as pets. It would be dangerous to rely on a Guide Dog which liked to chase them. Every puppy is introduced to a friendly cat in order to see what happens. A puppy unable to resist the temptation to annoy cats could not be relied upon.

Sudden and strange noises happen everywhere, and at all times of the day and night. No Guide Dog should ever be unduly frightened by them. Fire engines and ambulances ring bells or wail their sirens; bangs are very common in the streets and in the home; people drop plates and trays; corks pop out of bottles; balloons burst at parties; workmen drop heavy tools on the pavement; thunder suddenly cracks in the sky. A dog helping a blind person should not bolt or show terror at these times, for its owner might have a serious accident.

The reaction of each puppy to a sudden sound is tested by trainers in this way. A small pistol is fired so that it can be heard plainly. The puppy will, of course, be interested, but it should not show any real alarm. Friendly puppies, like Labradors and alsatians rarely do, but all doubts have to be removed for the safety of the blind.

[37]

A Puppy Walker talks to a new recruit

Finally, each puppy is tested to discover what happens if it is touched unexpectedly. Nobody can walk along the streets and not brush up against other persons or graze a wall or lamppost. Guide Dogs will be touched and pushed in the same way as humans. Pedestrians don't always make way for dogs, particularly in the rush and bustle of towns and cities.

The puppies are tapped on the sides of their bodies. If they jump away in surprise or shock, trainers know they would never be completely safe for blind people. If they pay no attention, they would be just as unsafe. A dog which was startled when touched might throw its blind master off balance, and a dog which never bothered if it brushed against a wall or tree would not take sufficient care of its blind owner. Happily, very few of the clever puppies fail to pass all the tests.

For the next part of their education the puppies go on a kind of holiday for a few months. It is important that each puppy should have the care and attention which only a family can give to it. As Guide Dogs live in ordinary homes with their blind owners, it is a great help if they have been a member of a family before they become real Guides. They learn what happens in a home, and what they should do and not do, just like small children with their parents. They then fit easily into a blind person's life and cause little trouble.

In the United States The Seeing Eye at Morristown find that the 4-H Club members in the surrounding counties are willing to help by providing homes for the puppies. Four-H

This Seeing Eye puppy is getting accustomed to being with all the family

Club young people (the 4-H's are Head, Heart, Hands and Health) bring up their lodgers under the expert guidance of The Seeing Eye. In Great Britain puppies are also placed in the care of families where there are children, who do the same for the Guide Dogs for the Blind. The people who do this are known as Puppy Walkers.

The puppies stay for six or seven months in their homes, after which they return to The Seeing Eye or the Training Centre from which they came. This is the story of what happened to one puppy in the North of England.

Tina was a yellow Labrador puppy who had passed all her tests and who was ready to go to a home. One day, a lady who had offered to have Tina, and so help a blind person, called to collect her. Mrs. White knew all about puppies like Tina, for she had taken a puppy once before.

" Tina is ready and waiting for you." A Supervisor greeted Mrs. White with a smile when she arrived in her car outside the puppy compound.

" I know you have had a puppy from us before, but here is a copy of our booklet which tells you what to do and how to care for her," she continued.

" Thank you very much. I will give it to my daughter. She was only a baby when we had the other puppy. She will be able to take more interest in Tina, and she will enjoy having a book of her own," Mrs. White replied.

" I will visit you as often as I can, and please inform me if you have any problems."

" I will. I want to be sure all goes well."

Mrs. White was delighted with Tina and her friendly welcome. She encouraged her into the car. She would need to practise getting in and out of vehicles.

" Make sure you tell us if she is travel sick," the Supervisor reminded her as they closed the door. Mrs. White nodded. She knew she mustn't be too soft-hearted. Travel-sick puppies would never do, for blind people relied on them to take them on buses and trains.

" I won't forget. I know that however much we love her you must know if we find anything wrong."

Mrs. White smiled as they began their short journey home. Tina took a lively interest in the noise and motion and seemed quite disappointed when the car drove up to the garage.

Mr. White and Susan, their daughter, were waiting with anticipation. Susan rushed to meet her mother and to say hello to Tina, and hardly stopped talking as they walked into the house. Her mother and father exchanged glances as they listened to her and noticed her great excitement.

" Now listen carefully, Susan," Mr. White spoke quietly, " Tina is not to be treated as an ordinary puppy. We must not spoil her, although she will have our affection. She will be here for only a short time before she goes to start her regular training lessons. We are to help her over her early weeks and watch for her good points and her weaker ones."

" Here is a little booklet which explains our job," her mother added.

[43]

Susan sat down with Tina in a large armchair and looked at the book. She was very quiet as her parents prepared a meal.

"Goodness me! What a lot there is to remember!" Susan looked at Tina with astonishment.

"Come and have something to eat. You can look at your book again later." Mrs. White beckoned her to the table. Susan ate in silence and as quickly as she could.

"We'll excuse you from wiping the dishes today, but we'll want to hear how much you know when we have finished," her father said.

When her parents returned and settled down on the settee they waited patiently for Susan to begin.

"Come on! You've had long enough." Mr. White puffed at his pipe.

"Well—Tina has to be taught to be house clean," Susan began hesitantly.

"Good! And what does that mean exactly?"

"She is not to make a mess in the house," Susan replied.

"Is that all?" Her mother raised her eyebrows.

"No, not all. She must not dirty the pavements but learn to use her special patch in the garden before she goes out and when she comes home."

"Regular clean habits. Very good," approved her father.

"And she must behave in the house and not jump up at visitors or frighten the tradesmen. She has to be well-behaved like her blind owner."

[44]

Teaching *Sit*. The left hand presses gently on the puppy's back

Teaching *Down*. Once again the leash
is held, to remind the puppy it is "on duty"

"Yes, that's right. She will have her play times, of course, when she can romp to her heart's content."

"Oh, yes!" remarked Susan. "She must know when she is 'on duty' and when she is 'off duty'."

"And how does she know that?" her father enquired.

"By always being attentive when her lead is on." Susan was pleased at remembering this.

"Excellent, Susan!" complimented her father.

Mrs. White smiled.

"She knows by the way we speak to her too. We must praise her when she is good, in a very pleasant voice," Susan continued.

"And speak sternly when we are displeased – 'Good girl' and 'Bad girl'! She soon spots the difference in our manner; that means you must never tease her. Puppies become excited when they are teased and may do something they shouldn't. Then they can't understand why you are cross so suddenly." Mr. White re-lit his pipe and settled back in his chair as he went on: "Tina will learn many things just by living here. We will stroke her and speak softly if she looks worried. Puppies like being spoken to kindly at such times. It won't happen often, of course – she wouldn't have been chosen if her nerves had been weak."

"Now, I think that's enough today. We must help her to settle down and get to know us." Susan's mother said.

During the week that followed the White family and Tina carried out all their tasks with great credit. Mrs. White had

[47]

most to do with the puppy as Susan had to go to school and Mr. White to work. When the Supervisor called one evening to see how Tina had settled down, Susan spoke as though she had done everything.

"And she was house clean very quickly, and she doesn't pull or lag behind on the lead, and she doesn't chase cats, and she isn't car sick, and—"

"Susan, perhaps the Supervisor wants to ask questions and not listen to a report on Tina's cleverness. It sounds as though she has no faults at all." Mr. White silenced his daughter's outburst.

"That's all right, Mr. White," their visitor said. "Perhaps your wife can tell me of any worries."

"Well, there *was* one thing at first. She began to display some excitement when she met other dogs. I think she's better now though."

"Why shouldn't she, Mummy?" Susan asked.

"Well, when she's out on the lead she must learn to concentrate. Too much attention to other dogs might be awkward. A blind person wouldn't know why she had stopped, and this would be a worry and a nuisance."

"Quite right," the Supervisor added. "Oh, it's quite permissible when she's having a romp, Susan, but she *must* attend when she is on the lead. I think you might begin her obedience exercises, somewhere away from any distractions. I will call again when I can."

"What excitement!" Susan said after the visitor had gone.

[48]

This pupil clearly knows what kind of shop it is

"May I read the instructions again about those exercises? I am afraid I can't remember what she has to do."

Mr. White handed her the booklet from the bookshelf. Susan sat on the floor and studied the exercises carefully.

She read that the puppies have to learn basic obedience exercises. These were very important and had to be done well, otherwise further progress would be delayed.

"It sounds rather like school," Susan thought.

Puppies had to be taught to *sit, down, stay* and *come*, on the given order. They must be praised by *good girl* when they tried hard and did well. The puppies should be trained in a place they knew well and then in quiet lanes or streets. Susan read on:

SIT   *No "tit-bits" should be given. Puppies should carry out orders willingly at all times. A Guide Dog must never expect a "tit-bit" as a reward. Its blind owner might run out of biscuits and his dog refuse to obey his order. This would never do! For* sit *the puppy should hear the order clearly. The puppy should be encouraged into position. The lead is held in the right hand while the left presses gently on its back. The hand is kept there for a few seconds before the puppy is allowed to rise. With regular practice she will remain, and should be praised when she does. After a few days the left hand can be taken away, while the puppy is stroked and spoken to kindly.* Sit

✳ –good girl. *The lead must be on as a precaution,*
and so that she knows she is " on duty ".

STAY   *This is taught when the puppy has been asked to*
sit. *The teacher should face the puppy at all times*
and walk a few steps away, gripping the lead. Stay –
good girl – stay. *As the puppy learns to* stay, *its*
teacher can go a step further away, and then wait a
few seconds longer. With practice and encourage-
ment the puppy will stay *for a minute or so with its*
teacher facing it.

DOWN   *Once again the puppy is asked to* sit. *With the lead*
in the right hand, as it always is, the teacher presses
gently on the puppy's haunches with the left. The
puppy is encouraged to the "down" position,
stroked, and spoken to kindly. When the puppy
knows what to do and doesn't try to rise, the left
hand can be taken away.

COME   *A puppy will* come *to its teacher when it is beckoned*
by the hand and encouraged. She should come to the
side and be asked to sit. *She should be patted and*
told she is a good girl *as soon as she takes up position.*

" Goodness me, what a lot to remember ! " Susan whispered
to Tina, who was lying at her side.

The family discovered that their puppy was quite quick to
learn, but she was always ready to stand up again. Training
had to be repeated often until she would stay in one position

[51]

by herself. They were delighted when she did, because they knew she could go into the quiet streets. She had to be reminded of her new exercises even when on walks. They took her into small shops and asked her to *sit* and *stay*. They told her what shop she was in.

"Butcher, Tina," Susan would announce proudly.

The young pupil really didn't need reminding of the smell of meat. She soon connected the word "Butcher" with the large marrow bone which was wrapped up for her.

Tina had become used to all the noises and bustle of town life. Cars speeding past hardly bothered her, neither did the sounds of railway trains or airplanes. She took a great interest in everything and many people came to know her. They also knew she was going to be a Guide Dog, because the family held her lead with their left hands. Although puppy obedience training is carried out with the lead held in the right hand, when the Guide Dog wears harness the blind person holds it in his left, so that his right hand is free. So, for walking, Susan and her family held Tina on their left.

Very soon Tina reached the age when it was time for her to begin her full training. Susan was disappointed and sad, but she was proud to feel that Tina would do well. She was not an ordinary puppy, she reminded herself. She was a very special puppy who was going to help somebody who needed her.

There was nothing more the White family could do. They all missed her a great deal, but they were pleased. They had done well, and Tina, perhaps, had done the best of all.

[52]

A future guide dog must be used to travelling

6: training the dogs

When the puppies return for their full training they are received with kindness and understanding. It is expected they may be upset for a day or two. They soon settle down and make friends, and there are opportunities for play with the other dogs. Then, in both Britain and the United States, this is what happens next.

As soon as a puppy is happy and contented again, it is taken for walks in the grounds. It is watched to see if it behaves on the lead. Then it is encouraged and coaxed to walk slightly ahead. All the dogs must do this in order to guide their blind owners. Each puppy is refreshed in obedience exercises to make certain it has been taught correctly.

[54]

A great deal of practice is given in changing direction, with gentle moves to the left, and then to the right. People do not always walk as straight as arrows. Blind people certainly don't. A puppy should be alive to the way human beings move, and learn how to keep close to the side of its owner. Very soon teacher and pupil begin to move together as a perfect example of team work.

After the puppies have received their refresher training, they are taken into quiet streets. Like small children, they have to be taught to cross roads. For future Guide Dogs this does not mean just looking to right and left to see if the roads are clear. They are taught that, at all times, they have to *stay* at the edge of a curb and wait for an order. All of the orders are short and easy to remember: *left – right – forward* and *stay*.

All this has to be practised frequently. The puppies need to do it so often that they are certain which way they have to go for *left* or *right*, or whatever the order is. It is amazing how quickly they learn, and when they have, they never make a mistake.

Qualified trainers now take charge. These are the men who have followed in the paths of Elliott Humphrey and Captain Liakhoff. They are experts, as men must be who train dogs to act as the eyes for the blind. As dogs need patience and special attention, each trainer looks after a small class, usually four at a time.

The first task is to introduce the young dogs to their smart harnesses and to the unusual handles which the blind person

[55]

A guide dog leads his owner safely around obstacles

grips. They are heavier than ordinary collars and leads and are put on the dogs with care. There is rarely any trouble, but the trainers do not hurry their dogs. They allow them to rest and play in their new harnesses and make friends with them before they clip on the handles. In Britain the harnesses and handles are white.

The next part of a dog's education is most interesting. Blind men and women are often at a loss in busy streets, and sometimes even in the country, because they never know whether they might walk into or stumble over a hard object in their path. Some blind people confess that this worry often makes them stay indoors.

The trainers teach their pupils how to help the blind around obstacles of this kind. There are many of them, but some of the most common are pillar boxes, telephone booths, lampposts, telegraph poles, signposts, trees, vehicles, ropes and bushes. One obstacle is met more than any other – pedestrians. People with normal sight may not realize that pedestrians are obstacles, but they are to the blind men and women who cannot see them. There is nothing more annoying than for two people to bump into each other.

The trainers, of course, know that clever dogs never walk into anything. They find a way around, just as human beings do. They need instruction, however, in leaving enough room for their future blind owners, as well as for themselves. They must be taught so well that they never forget to do this.

The first lesson usually takes place in the quiet grounds

near to the kennels. A tree, or a post, is chosen as an obstacle. The trainer walks around with the young dog in the usual way. She probably thinks they are just having a pleasant trip on the lawns and down the tracks. The trainer then takes her towards the tree, knowing she will go past it, but without leaving room for him. A blind person would certainly strike himself on the trunk of the tree. As the young dog prepares to go past, her trainer does three things, all at the same time. He pushes her further out to the side, strikes the tree with the palm of his hand, and calls out "No".

The young pupil is astonished by all this fuss. The sound of her trainer's hand on the tree attracts her attention. All very odd, she thinks.

She is even more astonished when exactly the same things happen when they approach the tree again. Her trainer sounds rather displeased, she reflects. Every time the pair try to pass the tree there is a reproval in her master's voice and actions. Well! There is only one thing to be done to prevent being pushed. A wider detour around the tree must be made.

"Good girl!" Her trainer showers her with praise. She wags her tail in delight as he strokes her. "Just take me around the lawn again," she seems to be saying. From that moment on, the movement is practised until her trainer knows the proud dog will always remember to provide room for him.

Obstacles are not always on, or near, the ground. Clothes-lines and the tops of doorways may be at the level of the blind

[58]

Trainers teaching dogs to stop at all curbs

person's chest or face. There are also low arches in some towns and cities, and scaffolding which workmen place across pavements. How does a dog know about these?

She must be taught about this too. When her trainer attracts her attention by knocking on something, and pushes her to the side calling out " No ", she has to make more room. Her trainer walks her towards the tree again, but this time goes up to an overhanging branch. As they come up close to it he slows down, raps on the branch, and calls out " No ".

She looks around for an obstacle and cannot find one near. The next time it happens she searches again to see what it is which is making her trainer say " No ". Sooner or later she notices the branch and knows what to do. She makes her way around it. In the future she is more aware of obstacles above.

Her trainer then takes her into the streets every day, so that she can meet as many obstacles as possible. Pedestrians are walking on the pavements, too, but the young dog is now confident about going around objects. She treats men, women and children in exactly the same way. If she goes too close to somebody, her trainer pretends to be upset. He sounds distressed, pauses, and rubs his leg. The dog is worried and sorry and rarely does it again. She likes her master too much to upset him.

By now the young dog is an expert on the pavements. There is only one thing left for her to do. She must be taught to cross from one side of the street to another and take care of her future blind owner in dangerous traffic.

[60]

Shows *Sit* position at curb while waiting to cross

The trainer knows that his pupil has no fear of cars. She has already had experience of the noises they make. His task is to teach her to view the noisy, moving vehicles as objects for which she must stop. Traffic signals are no help to dogs. On days of poor visibility they would not see them, and neither are they able to distinguish between one colour and another. They have to be taught what they should do before, and during the crossing of a busy street.

Two trainers are needed for the lessons. One drives a car and the usual trainer has the dog. They choose a quiet lane where there is little chance of any interruption. The first task is to make sure that the dog will not try to step off a curb when a car is coming along the road. Her trainer takes her to the edge where she *stays* as she has been taught. She will wait there for an order before she moves. When her trainer is ready he signals to his friend in the car. The car is started up and moves up the road towards them. The dog's trainer gives the order *forward*. Just as she is about to move, she is astonished to hear her master say " No " very clearly. He also grips her tightly and holds her back.

The car zooms up, making a loud noise, and then stops in front of them. It stops for a few seconds, and moves on. The dog's trainer then, and only then, allows her to cross. This drill is repeated many times, until she realizes she may hear the word *forward* and yet have to wait for a noisy moving vehicle to go past her.

This drill is also done when the dog has been given the

Two trainers teaching traffic drill

Pedestrians are used to seeing trainers with dogs
on the streets of Morristown

order *forward* and actually leaves the curb to cross. On her way across, however, the car approaches from the other direction. Once again her trainer says "No" and holds her back until it has gone. She is then allowed to finish her crossing.

The trainers try her out with a bicycle which moves with very little noise. She soon spots that it is moving and that she must wait for it to go. Once she has mastered a bicycle, her trainer takes her into the town and they practise on real cars, buses and bicycles. After this he knows that she will soon be ready to be the eyes of a blind man or woman.

For the last few days of their training, the dogs are taken into the busiest parts of the town. They are taken into shops and restaurants, where blind people will want to do their shopping and have a meal. The dogs are told which shop they are in. They have amazing powers of scent, and their noses tell them which shop they have entered.

They are taken on to buses so that they can learn how to lead their trainer on and off the platforms. They also learn to enjoy the ride, and not to be worried by the sound of the engine or the ringing of the bell.

Indeed, they are taken to all the places to which blind people are likely to go, including railway stations. When they have been two or three times they know what their trainer wants by the request "Railway Station – Good Girl".

All this preparation takes about four months. The dogs are then ready for the arrival of the blind men and women they are to help.

7 : a blind man's story

As soon as a number of dogs have completed their full training, blind men and women arrive at a Training Centre or
The Seeing Eye for a month's stay. They come to meet their
dogs and learn how to care for them and how to use them.

Each of them has a story to tell of how he felt and what his
stay meant to him. The story of Norman Walker concerns a
man who became blind unexpectedly, and who had never
owned a dog in his life, not even when he was a boy.

Before the war Norman Walker was living in a small town
not far from Liverpool in the North of England. He had just
started business as a cabinet maker. He and his wife were
looking forward to a happy life together.

During the war Norman Walker served as a soldier. Soon

after returning home and starting work again, he noticed that his eyesight was fading. It became so poor that he began to mistake windows for doors, and stumbled when he went up and down steps. It became so dangerous for him to visit people, especially in the dark days of winter, that he had to give up his business.

A doctor told him that he might become totally blind and that nothing could be done for him.

Mr. and Mrs. Walker decided to buy a small shop so that Norman could earn a living without having to go outdoors. Unfortunately, the doctor's words came true, for his eyesight became worse and he became blind. Mrs. Walker did all that she could to manage on her own, but her husband was so worried and upset that he began to lose hope. He was afraid of going out and stayed indoors day after day, week after week, and month after month.

The fear of moving around in the dark of his blindness forced the unhappy man to shuffle from room to room. His wife watched as he lost his appetite owing to a lack of exercise and fresh air. All her dreams and happiness seemed to have faded in the cruel misfortune of her husband's blindness.

One day Mrs. Walker was serving at the counter when a gentleman customer asked about her husband's health.

"He is blind, I'm afraid. The doctor says there is nothing that can be done. He won't go out, and stays indoors all day. He has no interest in anything. I have to do everything for him. I am really very worried about him."

[67]

First meeting with his future guide dog

" Have you ever thought about a Guide Dog? If you write to the Guide Dogs for the Blind and apply for a dog he will be out and about in no time."

" A Guide Dog! No, I never thought about that. We know nothing about dogs at all. I don't know what Norman will say, but I will suggest it to him. Thank you very much."

Mrs. Walker lost no time in telling her husband. She was pleased by his reply : " I have never had a dog in my life, but I will try anything. I can't bear living like this."

About six months later Norman was driven by his brother to the Training Centre in the North of England. He had a blind man's stick in his hand as he groped his way towards the entrance. He was made to feel very welcome, and all the staff showed great kindness to him. His first surprise was the complete absence of dogs. He had thought that there would be dogs everywhere, but for the first few days he only heard them barking outside somewhere in the distance. During the first weekend he met his trainer and attended lectures. He heard about Puppy Walking and the way the dogs were trained. He was told how to encourage his dog by his voice and kind manner, and never forget to praise her and tell her what a " good girl" she was. It all sounded very odd to the man who had never had a dog before !

The next morning his trainer led him outdoors into the grounds.

" I have a handle in my hand, exactly the same as the one you will find attached to your dog's harness. I want you to grip

[69]

one end of it in your left hand. I shall hold the other and pretend to be your dog. I am then going to lead you around the grounds at the speed of a dog. Do you understand, Mr. Walker? " his trainer asked.

"Yes, I think so," replied Norman, feeling rather puzzled.

"I will explain the reason for this afterwards. Ready? Off we go."

The "dog" moved off at a speed which Norman would have found easy before he was blind. Now he felt he was going like the wind, and he puffed along the path like an old man. His trainer allowed little rest, and asked him to give words of command as he would to his dog.

"Left," repeated Norman, and immediately his trainer set off and turned as a dog is trained to do. It seemed an age before they returned to the Training Centre, where Norman tried to recover his breath.

"Very good indeed," complimented the trainer. "I was testing you to find out how you walk. People walk in quite different ways, you know. This may surprise you, but it is true. I also wanted to find out how you give orders. Dogs are different, too. We have to find a confident dog for a confident person, and a quiet dog for a quiet person."

"What kind of dog shall I have?" asked Norman.

"Oh, a confident one."

The blind man felt pleased, but rather tired.

"I have a pleasant surprise for you now. If you will go to your room and wait there, I will bring your dog to you."

Students in the grounds of
the Seeing Eye house at Morristown

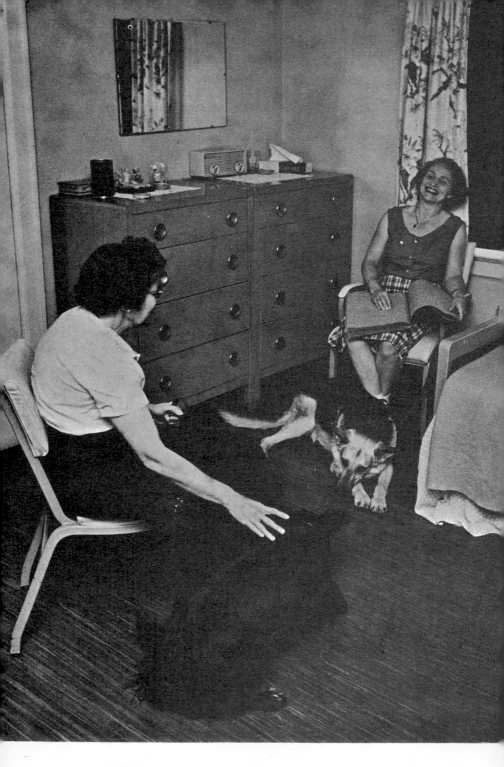

Students and dogs get accustomed to being together all the time

Norman was excited as he waited in his room. He heard the door open and knew she had arrived. His trainer introduced her to him.

"This is 'Speedy', Mr. Walker. She is a yellow Labrador retriever and is very beautiful. She will stay with you all the time, except for her evening meal and her nightly sleep in her kennel. I hope you make friends very quickly and will be happy together. Goodnight."

He was alone with the dog he couldn't see. He felt very strange. Speedy behaved as all friendly dogs can be expected to do. She approached Norman and quietly pushed her nose against his hand. He patted her head gratefully and whispered, "Good girl, Speedy – good girl."

The Labrador quickly gained a place in his heart. When his trainer returned later to take her to her kennel for the night, Norman knew somehow that they were going to get on well.

He returned to bed and fell asleep trying to picture the face of the dog he would learn to admire and love.

For the next few days Norman and three other blind students were taught how to give orders properly and how to talk to their dogs.

Speedy was very fond of the trainer. She often looked up at him as if to ask if her new master knew anything at all about dogs. The trainer had to remind Norman he must talk to Speedy often so that she would know he was her master.

"Mr. Walker, Speedy is not walking properly. She is

watching another dog across the street. Can't you tell by the slack harness that she isn't paying attention? Talk to her! "

"Come along Speedy. Hup – hup! " Norman reminded her.

"Good! " complimented his trainer. "You can feel the difference, I expect."

"Yes, I can," agreed the blind man.

That evening Norman's trainer told him that dogs were just like children. They could not be expected to give of their best unless they knew an interest was being taken in them. They needed encouragement, reminders, and praise when they had done well. His trainer told him a story of how one dog decided to teach her master a lesson. The dog worked well for many days and had never been praised by a single *good girl*. She walked, on purpose, very close to a lamppost so that her master would have a bump. He cried out in surprise and rubbed his legs. His trainer told him why his dog had done it. "She did it deliberately. Walk her again and talk to her and tell her what a clever girl she is," the trainer advised. The blind man did so, and the Labrador took him past the post quite safely.

"Good girl! " he cried thankfully. She wagged her tail with pleasure and pride. She knew he would never forget again.

Norman went outside into the quiet streets every day with Speedy. His trainer was never far away and watched as they

Many of the blind housewife's everyday jobs
can be undertaken with a guide dog

met obstacles and found their way around them. Once they went into a shop, and then had to find the door to make their way back into the street. This wasn't as easy as he had thought it would be. It was easier the second time when he had an idea where the entrance was and the position of the door handle.

One day the trainer told him that Speedy and he were doing so well that he would allow them to cross a road. They had never done this before. All of their training had been on the pavement and around corners. The thought of crossing the road in busy traffic was quite thrilling. He wondered if he would be nervous.

"It will not be a major crossing, Mr. Walker. We will choose a quiet place somewhere. You will need practice so that you will feel safe and confident. Speedy knows what to do. All you need to decide is when to tell her to cross. Listen carefully, and when you are sure there is nothing coming, say 'forward'. She will then take charge and you can leave everything to her. I will be near to you, of course."

The blind man did exactly as he was told. He waited with Speedy at the edge of the curb where the trainer had asked them to cross. He heard no noise of traffic and knew he must make his decision.

"Forward," he called, with a strong beating of his heart. Down into the road they stepped, and straight across to the other side they went, without anything happening at all.

"Marvellous!" he cried. "I haven't crossed a road alone for years."

[76]

"You did well, but you mustn't expect to cross so easily every time," commented his trainer.

Norman discovered that this was quite true. The following day they were crossing a road when Speedy suddenly stopped. There was the roaring of a vehicle which shot across their path. Speedy continued on her way. It was a wonderful experience to reach the other side, without any need to worry.

The end of the month's stay at the Training Centre came very quickly. Norman had been so busy, and so interested, that he could hardly believe he would soon be home.

"You may leave your white stick here if you wish," one of the staff said on the day of his departure. It was hard to realize he had needed a stick only a few weeks ago. He decided to leave it where it was and leave the past behind him. Speedy was his future, and his Labrador had no need of a white stick.

Mrs. Walker was waiting for him when he arrived home. The smile on his face told her all she wanted to know. It was the smile of a man who knew his life had been changed.

"You look so well," said Mrs. Walker.

"I am a different person," replied Norman Walker. Speedy looked up at him with the eyes that had brought new hope to her master.

Norman Walker is now a happy and confident man. He serves in his shop, does errands in the main street of the town, and recently had his first holiday for many years. Speedy took him on a fishing trip in Scotland. It is not impossible for a blind man to go fishing when he has a Guide Dog.

8: stories about guide dogs

BEAU

The first Guide Dog in Australia was called Beau, the French word for "handsome". His mistress was very proud of him and soon learned that he was a most unusual Guide Dog. Whenever she took him on their shopping visits, he was quick to find the places she wanted. After a few weeks her request for "Cake-shop" was answered by Beau immediately, and he was able to take her to the shop of her choice. She never had to ask for any help from passers-by, or find out if they were going in the right direction.

Beau did the same for "Post Office" and "Butcher". He

[78]

became so confident in shops that he began to show an ability to go to different counters. For example, in the Post Office, which was quite large and confusing for a blind lady, Beau was able to go to the stamp counter or parcels counter. His mistress only needed to say " Stamps, Beau " and off he would go to the place where she could be supplied.

After a year or two Beau became something of an expert in the town's large store. Not unlike those in the United States and Britain, it was a busy place, and shoppers moved impatiently from floor to floor, which were connected by escalators and lifts. Beau's keen ears helped his mistress to know which lift was going Up or Down. He astounded everybody waiting by showing no desire to enter if he knew it was going in the wrong direction. When it came back, he had no hesitation in guiding his mistress through the open doors.

When she had finished shopping, Beau's mistress had little trouble in returning home. Guide Dog owners often need to ask the direction to a bus stop when they have made their way out of shops into the main street. This never happened 'to Beau's mistress. All she had to remember was to say " Bus Stop " and her willing and clever Guide Dog took her to one.

· GRETA

Greta was born in the beautiful and sunny state of California, in the United States. She was also lucky enough to be trained there with a blind mistress who had travelled from northern

A collie dog guides its mistress confidently down steps

Missouri. The climate there is not always as reliable as in California, particularly in the winter.

When Greta had finished her training at The Guide Dogs for the Blind and began the long journey to her mistress's home, she had never had the experience of a bad winter. This is not very surprising, for she was only a litle over a year old. Even for lucky dogs, however, all good things sometimes come to an end.

About two years later, Greta and her mistress were fast asleep in the friendliness and warmth of their home. Outside, and unknown to them, it was snowing very heavily, and already there was a thick covering in the streets and gardens.

Snow and ice often bring traffic to a halt, interfere with power supplies, slow down rail and air services, and handicap farmers. Pedestrians find the conditions trying and exhausting, but they rarely become lost or confused. A blind person is completely dependent on the Guide Dog, and after a heavy fall of snow the work of a dog is seriously affected. The edges of pavements have disappeared; roads and pavements look exactly the same, and well-trodden and familiar paths cannot be seen.

The blizzard in that part of Missouri had lasted for a few hours only, but its effects were to remain for some days. When Greta and her mistress had finished breakfast, and were preparing to go to their work in the town, they expected difficulties. One, however, was quite exceptional.

This boxer dog carefully leads its master
around an open manhole

On their way into town there was a deep ditch and the only way to cross was over a narrow wooden bridge. After many trials and anxieties in the snow and both feeling rather weary and worried, Greta and her mistress approached the ditch. Unfortunately, the snow had altered the whole appearance of the spot. The ditch was filled in by drifts and banks of snow and looked no different from the rest of the area. The wooden steps to the bridge had been buried.

Surrounded on all sides by snow, which she had never seen before in her life, and unable to see any trace of the ditch or the steps to the bridge, Greta was lost. The Guide Dog was not going to admit defeat, nor was she going to disappoint her mistress, who relied on her ability.

Greta raised her head to search for a view of the bridge itself. This was still visible, as it was too high to be buried. It looked different, of course, but Greta felt sure it was the bridge. She guided her mistress towards it. Then she began to whimper and paw at the snow. Her mistress realized that her dog had taken her to a place where she needed some help. Her whimpers and frantic pawing were meant to tell her something. Surely Greta was asking her to clear the snow for her!

Dog and mistress worked slowly together. Greta could see the bridge and nosed and pushed her blind mistress in its direction. On her hands and knees, her mistress cleared a rough path for her dog. It was a cold and tiring task. After some minutes of effort, they both found what they had been

[83]

searching for – the edges of the first step which led up to the bridge. Mistress and dog crossed in safety.

VANGY

Vangy was a boxer bitch who lived with her mistress near to an underground railway station at East Ham, in London. Boxers are very popular dogs in Britain and the United States. Vangy was one of the best of her breed, as her story shows.

Her mistress had a friend whom she had known for many years. They frequently visited each other, for they lived in the same district, and spent many of their holidays together. After a number of years of companionship the friend had moved to another part of London. It was not a very long journey by the London Underground, and Vangy's mistress was looking forward to visiting the new home as soon as her friend had settled down.

The clerk at the East Ham station advised her to travel near to the front of the train. They had to change trains at Mile End station. When they got out she would find the staircase leading to the other trains quite near. Vangy's mistress was grateful for the advice and thanked the kindly clerk.

Mistress and boxer Guide Dog waited for their train and were able to board the first compartment. The clerk had told her how many times the train would stop and which one would be Mile End. She counted the stops carefully and then stood near to the doors, ready to step out. All compartment doors on the underground railway open and close automatic-

[84]

ally. When the doors were heard to open, Vangy's mistress asked her to go *forward*.

Much to her surprise, Vangy didn't move. At first, the blind lady thought her dog had lost her concentration and had failed to hear her. She repeated the order, making it louder so that there could be no mistake. Vangy remained stubborn and wouldn't obey. She coaxed and pleaded, but to no avail. Then, as she had expected, the doors closed and the train moved out of Mile End for the next station.

When the train stopped again Vangy had forgotten all about her lack of obedience and was only too ready to leave the train. When the blind lady was standing on the platform and searching inside her handbag for her ticket a gentleman spoke to her.

" Excuse me, but I saw you trying to leave the train at the last station. I was watching from the next compartment. How amazing it was for your dog to know! "

Vangy's mistress was not sure what he meant and asked him.

" Why, your compartment had overshot the platform. If your dog had led you through the open door you might have been killed on the lines."

Vangy was very pleased to hear what a good girl she was!

SUNNY

Sunny, a harvest golden Labrador, lives in central England. Her mistress had never owned a dog before she became blind. When she took Sunny back home after they had finished their training, she was still not sure if a dog would not be more trouble than it was worth. Dogs, even Guide Dogs, cannot feed themselves, groom themselves, or be left alone when they are ill. Her friends, who were very fond of her and always ready to help her, were anxious for her safety. They could not really believe that a dumb animal could look after a human being. They believed their friend would have an extra worry in a life already affected by blindness.

For the first few days Sunny wasn't taken far. Her mistress put on her harness when she needed to visit a friend, but as she hadn't to cross any roads and knew her way, her Guide Dog had really very little to do.

One day everything was changed. Someone living close by called at Sunny's home to tell her mistress that she had received a telephone message for her. A relative had been taken ill and the family wanted her to telephone for news at nine o'clock that evening. Sunny's mistress had no telephone of her own and occasionally was brought messages in this way.

Unfortunately, it was already evening and she had no chance to arrange for anybody to take her to a telephone. The friend who brought the message had to go out that evening and couldn't help either. There was only one solution: she would have to use Sunny and find a public telephone booth. She had never had to go out by herself after nightfall and, although she had some idea where to find a public telephone, she couldn't help feeling nervous.

Allowing herself what she thought was plenty of time, the

Department Store shopping at leisure and without help

blind woman dressed Sunny in her harness and went out into the street. It was drizzling with rain and very few people were out, but she did hear a few cars now and then. In her shock of the news of her relative, the Guide Dog owner had forgotten her fears about crossing roads. Suddenly she realized that Sunny had taken her safely across three!

Continuing on her way, the anxious woman arrived in the area where she knew there was a telephone booth. She held out her right hand and groped on all sides, but she couldn't find it. She heard a pedestrian coming along the street and decided to ask exactly where it was. Perhaps the person would be kind enough to take them to it.

"I wish I could help you, but I am a stranger to the district," the man replied, and went on his way. She hadn't told him she was blind and he didn't seem to know. Blind owner and Guide must have looked like any ordinary person and dog. She was pleased about this. It was wonderful to know that her handicap was not obvious any more.

"Goodness me!" thought the blind woman, "it must be nearly nine o'clock and we still haven't found the telephone." She was lost and helpless. There was only Sunny able to help, but she was a stranger to the district, too, and had never been asked to go quite as far before. In desperation, however, Sunny's mistress called, "Find me the telephone. Find the telephone, Sunny."

Off went the golden Labrador in the opposite direction. Her mistress thought that she must have confused her dog and that she was returning home. After a few minutes or so Sunny stopped and refused to go. Her owner was puzzled by this action, for she knew they hadn't walked far enough to have reached home. She felt around her with her hand again and, to her joy and amazement, felt the rough surface of the outside of a public telephone box.

"Find me the door, Sunny – to the door." The Guide Dog immediately moved, and guided her a few more steps. Feeling around once more, the blind woman's hand made contact with a glass door. They both went inside.

Sunny's owner never doubted her dog's ability after that evening.

VOLLY

Another story concerns a blind man and a male dog, Volly. Every day, whatever the weather, Volly took his master to work through the busy Kilburn High Road in London. They had never once been late, not even in heavy rain or thick fog.

One day their daily journey was made much more difficult. The Highways Department arrived and began to remove portions of the pavements so that they could repair the drains. Volly was not at all worried and took the workmen's activities in his stride. He picked his way very carefully around the picks and the shovels and guided his master safely. They still arrived at their work on time. The workmen stopped to watch him for the next few days, but they soon became accustomed to his skill in avoiding their tools and equipment.

One morning the men waited for Volly's approach with much more interest and an air of excitement. The Guide Dog and his master came along the road at their usual time, but the blind man soon knew that there was a difference. There was a sway under his feet at certain places, and he had the sensation of walking on a board or plank. A murmuring of voices told him that they had done something unusual.

"Well done, indeed," a strange but friendly voice said. "There was only just enough room for both of you." Volly, he was told, had guided him over three narrow wooden planks which had been placed across deep trenches.

Continuing on his way with a proud owner, Volly gave him yet another surprise by turning left at a place where they usually went straight ahead. By doing this he ignored a street which was on their normal route to work. The blind man trusted his Guide and allowed him to go on. Volly then turned right as though he was making a circle to get back on to the street he had avoided before. This proved to be true, for they arrived at work without being late.

The following evening he was full of his Guide Dog's deeds and behaviour and told all his friends. The local policeman was most impressed. Volly's circle had been necessary, he said, because his usual street was blocked to all traffic and pedestrians by repair work. Volly had certainly remembered his early obstacle training.

Seeing Eye dogs and their owners have had their share of

amusing and heroic stories. It must always be remembered, however, that Guide Dogs are trained and expected to lead their owners in safety. Many of their deeds are heroic because they are doing their jobs well. One of the last tests for a Seeing Eye dog is to see if it can make wise decisions of its own. The dog has to take the owner wherever it is asked – in complete safety!

Even so, there are sometimes one or two happenings which are unusual. One took place on a wintry morning when a young blind woman decided to do some shopping. She knew that the pavements were icy and that walking with her dog would be difficult, as a number of her sighted friends had told her to go carefully. They had slipped on the smooth layers of ice and snow.

The morning air was very sharp and refreshing. The young woman soon forgot her fears as she walked proudly down the street with her Seeing Eye dog. Arriving at a street corner, she listened carefully for any sound of traffic before she gave the order *forward*. Her dog looked with his keen eyes to make sure all was safe, and then began to cross over to the other side of the street.

Suddenly, and without any warning, the young woman slipped on a glassy patch and sat down with a bump. Her face was a picture of unbelief and shock.

The dog was as surprised as his mistress, but the noise of a car coming around a corner didn't give him time for sympathy. Something had to be done, and at once. The Seeing

Eye dog braced himself, leaned on the harness, and pulled with grim determination. He expected that his mistress would be a heavy load. He had forgotten what had caused her to slip – the smooth ice! His blind owner glided swiftly across the street as though riding a sledge in the frozen North.

The dog stopped triumphantly at the other side, and waited to hear the praise he had earned. Nearby pedestrians, who had been horrified at the sight of a helpless woman in the path of a car, saw the funny side of the incident. The young woman began to laugh. The Seeing Eye dog appeared to have a grin on his face. Soon everybody was roaring with laughter.

Not all dangerous situations end in mirth. One Seeing Eye dog, whose owner was a blind man, took part in an exciting story which happened in a hotel. Away from traffic, and in a comfortable building which they knew well, there was no reason to think that anything unusual would happen.

One day the dog and his master left their room, which was on one of the higher floors, to go down to ground level by the lift. The blind man was familiar with the building. He knew how to find his way, and the dog also knew what he had to do. When the lift stopped and the door opened the dog took his master inside. No order was needed.

The man was led to the lift as usual, and waited for it to arrive. He heard the door open and expected his dog would lead him inside as he always did. On this occasion, however, the Seeing Eye dog didn't move. His master ordered him to go forward, but the dog held his ground. As he was becoming

[92]

impatient with this disobedience a chambermaid walked to-wards them. She saw the blind man trying to persuade his dog to go forward and screamed in terror.

The door was wide open but the lift was not there! A mechanical fault had opened the door on to the open shaft.

If the dog had obeyed his master they would have fallen down the shaft and been killed.)

The blind men and women in these stories are only a few of the thousands who have cause to be grateful to their dogs. Through the efforts of the Seeing Eye and the Guide Dogs for the Blind their lives have been changed. Many of their former joys have returned and some new ones have been gained.

The dogs guide their blind owners in the countryside and in large towns and cities in many lands. There are dogs help-ing the blind in Australia, South Africa, Greece, Germany, Canada, Israel, Switzerland, France, Italy, Holland, Britain and the United States.

Guide Dogs render their noble service for as long as they are fit and capable. When they become old, and their hearing, eyesight and swift judgements are not as good as formerly, they are retired like other faithful servants. Their owners are re-trained with younger pairs of eyes and the older dogs are kept as pets.

There is, then, no ending to the story of the Willing Walkers. Young dogs take over from the old and tired ones, while others assist men and women who have never had dogs before. The brisk steps of a blind person being led by a large dog in a special harness is the sign of a happy friendship. Such confidence and trust are reminders that, by patience, determination and courage, it is possible to make a fresh start in life. Success can be achieved, even when failure is thought to be close at hand.

All owners of Guide Dogs believe that they own the best dogs in all the world. In a way, each is right, and surely no sighted owner would ever disagree with them.

index

[95]

index

Printed by Gilmour & Dean Limited, Hamilton and London